# HAPPY BIRTHDAY

## TO

..................................................

## WITH LOVE FROM

..................................................

*And Joan*

# HAPPY BIRTHDAY—LOVE . . .
## Complete Series

Jane Austen

Joan Crawford

Bette Davis

Liam Gallagher

Audrey Hepburn

John Lennon

Bob Marley

Marilyn Monroe

Michelle Obama

Jackie Kennedy Onassis

Elvis Presley

Keith Richards

Frank Sinatra

Elizabeth Taylor

Oscar Wilde

# HAPPY BIRTHDAY
## Love, Joan

ON YOUR SPECIAL DAY

ENJOY THE WIT AND WISDOM OF

## JOAN CRAWFORD

THE WORLD'S MOST TERRIFYING DIVA

Edited by Jade Riley

CELEBRATION BOOKS

THIS IS A CELEBRATION BOOK

Published by Celebration Books 2023
Celebration Books is an imprint of Dean Street Press

Text & Design Copyright © 2023 Celebration Books

All Rights Reserved. No part of this publication may be reproduced, stored in or transmitted in any form or by any means without the written permission of the copyright owner and the publisher of this book.

Cover by DSP

ISBN 978 1 915393 54 8

www.deanstreetpress.co.uk

# HAPPY BIRTHDAY—LOVE, JOAN

From a dirt poor childhood to second-string Broadway chorus girl and finally on to screen goddess, Joan Crawford worked her way up to top billing just by doing just that: work! Although her talent and good looks came naturally, her determination was unstoppable. Still Hollywood eats talented, pretty girls for breakfast. So how did Joan do it? Unwavering self belief. In New York City, she was picked by Louis B. Mayer from a back row of dancers to go out to his California studio. When she got there, there was no one to help her. At the time, actors did their own make-up so little Joan created her own signature look. There were no parts for her besides extra-work, so she spent evenings at dance contests in Hollywood nightclubs like the Coconut Grove just to get noticed. A smart cookie, Joan made fun part of her career moves!

And the roles came her way. And she slowly became a leading lady. But it was when she met and married Hollywood royalty, Douglas Fairbanks Jr., that life became a little sweeter for Joan. She could finally enjoy the party. Ever the giver, Ms. Crawford preferred to host the party. Later, she wrote a book about how to live graciously and entertain. Joan even had one special trick to make sure everyone had a great time: "always add a splash of vodka to everything . . . Nobody ever knows; everyone ends up having a wonderful time."

Dozens of photos feature Joan celebrating birthdays with the most enormous cakes. But isn't it interesting that in Paris, famous society hostesses wanting to give their guests a special treat, would finish the evening by showing a Joan Crawford movie. It's no surprise—Joan Crawford was the party!

*Joan Crawford*

"Be afraid of nothing."

"I need sex for a clear complexion, but I'd rather do it for love."

"Love is a fire. But whether it is going to warm your hearth or burn down your house, you can never tell."

If I can't be me, I don't want to be anybody. I was born that way.

I believe in the dollar. Everything I earn, I spend!

Hollywood is like life, you face it with the sum total of your equipment.

"I think the most important thing a woman can have—next to talent, of course—is her hairdresser.

 Make the camera adore you.

# Be a giver, not a taker.

"I've persuaded myself that I hate things that are bad for me – fattening food, late nights, and loud and aggressive people head the list.

"I'm friends with myself, so I do things that are good for me, otherwise I couldn't be good for others.

"I never go outside unless I look like Joan Crawford the movie star. If you want to see the girl next door, go next door.

Women are lucky, I think, because they can get so much more variety into their lives than most men can.

"I'm so normal that it hurts."

"Learn to breathe,
learn to speak,
but first . . .
learn to feel."

Being cheerful on the phone is part of giving. Sure, we all have our problems, but why inflict them on our friends?

I was a strict disciplinarian, perhaps too strict at times, but my God, without discipline what is life?

"There is nothing shameful about the pursuit of knowledge.

"Scrubbing, for me, is the greatest exercise in the world. It gives me rosy cheeks, and I just have a ball.

"I love playing bitches. There's a lot of bitch in every woman—a lot in every man."

"Someone tore off my warning label when I was born.

"I never touch sweets. I'd much rather have a dill pickle."

A parent has to guide, advise, educate, and love. If they are sure of the love, they'll accept the guidance.

"Not that anyone cares, but there's a right and wrong way to clean a house."

"Women's Libbers always look so unhappy. Have you noticed how bitter their faces are?

# Find your happiest colors—the ones that make you feel good.

"My tears speak for me."

"If you throw a lamb chop in the oven, what's to keep it from getting done?"

Beautiful clothes look awful draped over a shapeless from. A really good figure can wear a twenty-dollar dress with verve.

There is more to marriage than sex—mind you, I'm not knocking it—but love is infinitely more than that.

"Don't you dare ask God to help me.

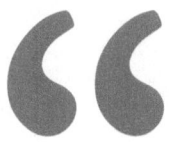

"If you've earned a position, be proud of it. Don't hide it. I want to be recognized.

'When in doubt, don't,' is never so true as when it comes to clothes. Or getting married.

"Taste does not come to a woman overnight.

I'm not disillusioned about marriage. It is still the most perfect state for man and woman.

 All the younger people I know are bright and attractive and have something to say.

I die a thousand deaths a day from timidity and indecision.

"The best parties are a wild mixture.

Care for your clothes like the good friends they are.

"An actor who's been around a while doesn't win an award for just one picture. There has to be an accumulation of credits.

A home-bound woman who depends on bridge clubs and shopping sprees for amusement has only half a personality.

Working is the best way of being completely fulfilled. And that's the kind of woman who makes her husband happiest.

The intelligent woman adapts herself to fashion, but never to fad. She knows what is best for her, and sticks to it.

I think that a woman
usually outgrows
a fragrance every
decade or so.

A woman who has married and brought up children has had a thousand emergencies, and has trained herself to take them all in stride.

Closets should be completely emptied twice a year.

"You have to live with a painting as you do with a lover.

"I think by nature a woman is more stable.

I heard a story that I had a party for twenty-five men. It's an interesting story, but I don't know twenty-five men I'd invite to a party.

"Sensitive husbands don't like second billing.

"

If you have an ounce of common sense and one good friend you don't need an analyst.

Some 'experts' tell you to diet five days a week and take the weekends off. I guess that's all right if you don't go berserk with chocolate éclairs and beer on Saturday and Sunday.

So many men like gooey, sweet things. Pander to them, and let them worry about their waistlines.

"Every woman tries to be a good mother, and then wonders if, after all her best efforts, her children will wind up on a headshrinker's couch complaining about bad treatment."

"I honestly believe there is no limit to success.

"

Conquering fears, whatever they may be, opens life up—and this life should be as full of different experiences as we can make it.

"This is a man's world and a girl has to fight for everything she wants.

Charm is not only being soft-spoken, relaxed, and at ease; it's wanting to be a giver.

> The higher you rise, the more is expected of you.

> Charm is a touch of magic. Try to make it a part of your way of life.

Choose your clothes for your way of life.

I had always known what I wanted, and that was beauty . . . in every form . . . a beautiful house, beautiful man, a beautiful life and image.

When I plan a menu I consider color, texture, taste, and balance.

Bitterness and self-pity are deadly poisons that can't be hidden. They seem to exude from the pores.

It was a man who taught me that the admission of error is an integral part of character.

"When eyebrows came back a lot of girls found that they couldn't grow them anymore.

To have a friend you have to be one. You have to learn to like yourself—which usually means getting over a few bad habits.

When I make a date with anyone, male or female, that date is kept. I value friendship too highly to endanger it.

"I sit on hard chairs—soft ones spread the hips.

"

 Everybody has strong ideas about marriage. And why not? It's the most intriguing situation a woman has in this life.

Moisturizer is probably the most blessed invention of the past two decades.

I feel as if clothes are people.
When I buy a dress, or buy
the fabric to have one made,
that's a new friend. Am I to
let it hang there and not give
it warmth and affection?
'Course not!

If every woman could walk into her husband's office and see how many beautiful women pass his desk every day, it would give her something to think about.

All the beauty products in the world can't disguise a disagreeable expression. Have you ever noticed that when you say 'no' you begin to resemble a prune-faced schoolmarm?

I surround myself with happy colors—yellow, coral, hot pink, and Mediterranean blues and greens.

"I made my girls give their hair the old-fashioned hundred strokes every night, using two brushes, and bending forward from the waist. It stimulates hair grows, and the rush of blood to the face is an added benefit.

No working relationship can be based on the premise, 'Me—woman; you—man!' It's 'we two' trying to make a job better.

"No man with low blood sugar ever comes to a happy agreement about anything.

There's nothing less stimulating for a man than the day-to-day business of raising four children. That's woman's work. If she's lucky she revels in it. If not, she gets it done anyhow, and in the time allotted for it.

Love can spring out of a need for security—not financial security, but the security of being wanted, adored. That's why women can give so much.

Never let your husband see you exercising. No woman rolling around on the floor looks really adorable after she's passed her third birthday.

A lot of other women are flirting with your husband and flattering him—you can depend on that.

Enjoying something first-rate together is the most satisfying experience anyone can have—be it sex or a symphony, it's good and it's shared.

"You can't be Shirley Temple on the Good Ship Lollipop forever. Sooner or later, dammit, you're old."

My God, I'm four hundred years old and the most I can do is look three hundred.

"Send me flowers while I'm alive. They won't do me a damn bit of good after I'm dead."

*Joan Crawford*

## ABOUT THE EDITOR

Jade Riley is a writer whose interests include old movies, art history, vintage fashion and books, books, books.

Her dream is to move to London, to write like Virginia Woolf, and to meet a man like Mr. Darcy, who owns a vacation home in Greece.

www.ingramcontent.com/pod-product-compliance
Lightning Source LLC
Chambersburg PA
CBHW030047100526
44590CB00011B/358